Superfoods

by Vaishali Batra

OXFORD
UNIVERSITY PRESS
AUSTRALIA & NEW ZEALAND

The Food We Eat

What food do you like?

Is it something you eat every day?

Food is the fuel that runs our bodies. It gives us **energy** to learn, play and grow. The choices we make about what we eat can make our bodies feel good or make us feel unwell.

The food we eat every day is called our diet.

Nutrients

The parts of food that our body uses are called nutrients. There are several kinds of nutrients and they have different jobs.

All these foods have different nutrients.

We need to eat a **range** of different foods to get the right nutrients and stay healthy. This is called a balanced diet.

Carbohydrates

The nutrients in cereals, bread, pasta and rice are carbohydrates. They are an important element of our diet. They give us energy to move and play.

About half the energy we get from our diet should come from eating carbohydrates.

Proteins

The nutrients in eggs, nuts, beans, meat and fish are called proteins.

Our body's **cells** are made up mainly of protein. We need protein to make new cells when we grow and to repair damaged cells.

Between 10% and 15% of our diet should be protein.

Fats

The nutrients in nuts, oils and dairy foods are fats. They give us energy to grow and keep us warm.

A small amount of fat provides us with a large amount of energy, so we only need to eat a little bit to get enough.

A balanced diet includes a small amount of these fats.

Vitamins

Vitamins are nutrients that help our body work properly. There are 13 different kinds. We only need small amounts, but they do important jobs for us.

These foods all contain vitamins.

Different foods have different vitamins. When we eat a variety of foods, we can get all the vitamins our body needs.

Vitamin A

B Vitamins

Vitamin C

Vitamin D

Vitamin E

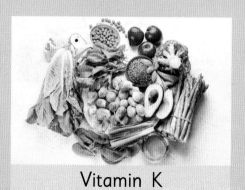
Vitamin K

Minerals

Minerals we get from our food help our body grow and stay healthy.

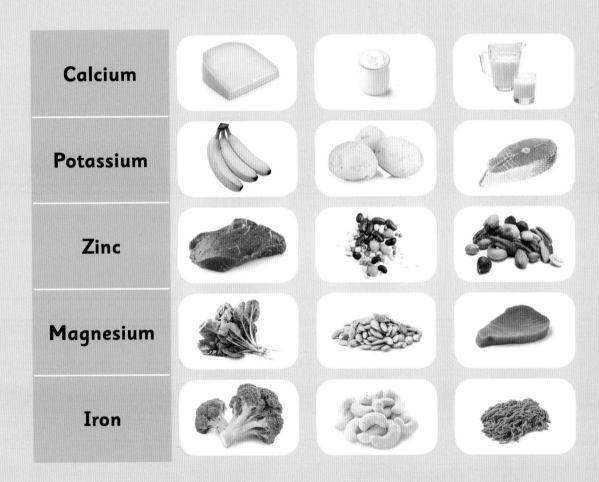

Calcium			
Potassium			
Zinc			
Magnesium			
Iron			

Some minerals help build parts of our body.

Calcium helps make strong bones and teeth.
Potassium helps our blood stay healthy.

Dairy foods like milk contain lots of calcium.

The Right Balance

Not all foods have the same nutrients. By eating lots of different foods, our body can get all the nutrients it needs. It is good for us to prepare and eat more foods that are full of nutrients.

Fruits and vegetables are colourful foods we can enjoy every day.

We can eat dairy foods such as milk, cheese and yoghurt **regularly**. They have proteins and minerals.

Some foods taste good, but don't give our bodies many nutrients. We should eat things like cakes and lollies only sometimes.

Save these foods for special occasions.

Superfoods

Some foods are packed with nutrients.
We call them **superfoods**!

Blueberries

Vitamins	A, C, K	
Minerals	potassium, manganese	
Good for	✓ skin ✓ hair ✓ eyes ✓ bones	✓ teeth ✓ blood ✓ muscles

Blueberries are packed with vitamins and minerals.

Try blending them into a juice for breakfast or adding them to a fruit salad for dessert.

Avocados ✓

Vitamins	C, E, K	
Minerals	magnesium, potassium	
Good for	✓ bones ✓ skin	✓ brain ✓ heart

We can have avocados several times a week. Their buttery **texture** makes them easy to spread on toast for breakfast.

You can also have avocado in **sushi** for lunch or in a salad for dinner.

Kale

Kale is a dark green leafy vegetable. It is one of the healthiest foods we can include in our diet.

You can use kale in a smoothie for breakfast, eat it raw in a salad, or steam it for dinner.

Vitamins	A, B, C, K		
Minerals	iron, calcium, magnesium, potassium		
Good for	✓ brain ✓ heart	✓ blood ✓ bones	✓ eyes ✓ skin

Kale makes delicious soup!

Walnuts ✓

Vitamins	B, E	
Minerals	copper, phosphorus, manganese	
Good for	✔ brain ✔ heart ✔ bones	✔ skin ✔ blood

Walnuts contain lots of nutrients and fats.

They are great for snacking on and they add a delicious crunch to salads.

Some people call walnuts **brain food**!

Beans

There are lots of types of beans, including chickpeas, lentils and kidney beans. They are very good for us.

Add them to a wrap for lunch, or have them in a stew for dinner.

Vitamins	B	
Minerals	iron, potassium, magnesium	
Good for	✓ brain	✓ blood

Mix up different beans in a salad for a tasty lunch.

Superfood Swap Challenge

Use the challenge checklist on the next page and take the superfood swap challenge.

- Can you try swapping less nutritious foods for superfoods?
- What superfoods could you have instead of chips or sugary cereal?
- Do you notice a difference in how you feel?

Challenge checklist

	Less nutritious foods	Nutritious foods
Breakfast	sugary cereal	avocado on toast
Lunch	chicken nuggets	bean wrap
Dinner	burger	kale salad
Dessert	ice cream	yoghurt
Snack	chips	nuts
Snack	lollies	blueberries

The right foods help our bodies grow and work the best they can. If we include a variety of foods in our diet, we can get all the nutrients we need to feel great.

Which foods will you choose?

Glossary

brain food: food with nutrients that help keep the brain healthy

cells: the building blocks of our bodies

energy: a person's strength and ability to do things

range: a collection of different things of the same type

regularly: happens often

superfoods: foods with lots of nutrients that help to keep our mind and bodies healthy

sushi: a Japanese dish of raw fish with rice

texture: the way that the surface of something feels

Index